D1247155

College Chapels

ISBN - 978-0-9571536-1-5

Published By Project and Management Solutions
First edition - 2012
Inquisitive.one@gmail.com

College Chapels

Greg J. E. Dickens

LIGHT's an interesting thing.

It ignites that internal argument between the physicist parts of the brain and the artist. The physicist, excited by visible examples of wave/particle duality, the notion of the Speed of Light, the idea of pigments and refractive colours. The artist, sobbing in joy and frustration at the play over forms and texture, the shadows that ink themselves out of the picture, the dazzling colours that draw the eye.

The biology of the situation is a third aspect and, to me, it is the most interesting. There is always too much and too little light in an image. Looking at a scene, some areas will contain so much light that the eye and the brain can only register them as white; while some areas will contain so little that the brain must understand them as black. However, if the eye is moved, making the brightest area the centre, the eye adapts. The pupil closes a bit, the levels of chemicals in the retina change, the brain shifts gear a bit and we come to see detail and contrast where nothing but white was visible before. The same occurs for black regions.

And this happens all the time, the eyes are constantly flicking around an image changing, recalibrating and working hard so your brain can sit back and enjoy the beauty of the scene. The problem comes when you try to pin that image down in a photograph. A photo has to be set at one level of exposure and you can't look around the image, changing the level of light as you go.

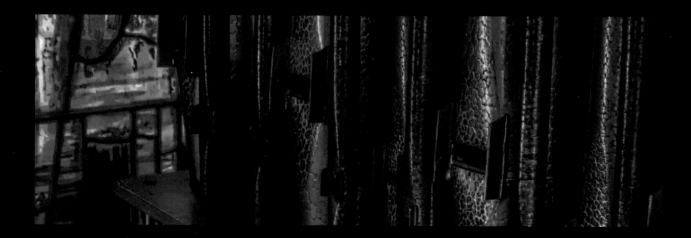

Chapels have a lot of dark and light areas. Their construction is in devotion to an ideal and so, they have features and details that most buildings do not. Light streams in abundance from detailed stained windows, dark and shadowy ceilings rest high above the ground. Simply put, they are built with love. This makes them very difficult to photograph. I wanted to show how these places of worship and contemplation look in total, not in a single exposure captured by a normal camera.

To do so, I have modified a technique used in medical X-radiography, the images were shot at multiple exposures to create a selection of start images. These were then compiled so that each pixel in the final image was chosen from the single start image that was correctly exposed in that area, hence, preserving the detail in the whole image.

This is how the chapels of Cambridge University look to me...

Ps. On the following pages you'll find every one of Cambridge University's 23 College Chapels. The Deans and Chaplains of those 23 have been kind enough to write a piece describing their favourite detail in their respective chapels. I have included this to add a layer of detail that could not be captured by the photos.

Also, I've thrown a short comment onto each page describing why the photograph has been created the way it has. Hopefully, this will answer some questions and give the final image a level of relevance in the overall collection - GJED

Gonville and Caius College

Caius Chapel is a beautiful place to pray, and there is much to catch and delight the eye, but one monument in particular stands out. A 17C memorial to a former Master, Thomas Legge, it records his friendship with one of the Fellows, John Gostlin, who later went on to become Master of the College. This epitaph takes the form of a Latin elegiac couplet:

Junxit amor vivos sic jungat terra sepultos. Gostlini reliquum cor tibi Leggus habes.

Which can be rendered:
Love joined them living; let earth now join them in the tomb.
Legge, you have the heart of Gostlin left to your keeping.

This inscription is itself a beautiful tribute to their close friendship. Even more moving is the symbol at its centre - a single flaming heart held by two hands. Perhaps, as the inscription might suggest, they are both the hands of Legge, holding the heart of Gostlin for ever; or perhaps they represent the two men with but a single heart, joined in that intimate friendship for eternity.

Rev'd Dr Cally Hammond

Caius strikes a balance between areas of amazing texture with subtle colours and a space with an overall dark and cool quality. I hoped that this view would reflect both of these facets - GJED

St Catharine's College

Replacing an earlier 16th century
building and dedicated in 1704,
the Chapel of St Catharine's
College is remarkable in that its
simplicity and austerity lend it
such intimacy and dignity.

It is a space of comfortable
yet powerful encounter and an
aweful silence is one of its most
dynamic architectural features.

At once lofty and light,
embracing and shadowy-detailed,
with the striking contrast of
upper level plasterwork and a
lower band of warmth-breathing
wooden panelling, the Chapel
invites one to fill the space with
thought, prayer and human
vulnerability and know that all is
secure within the love of God.

Rev'd Dr Anthony Moore

Catz has a lot of light and lot of
very shiny surfaces. Both of
which give it an airy feeling
under gentle winter lighting.

This piece of detailed metalwork
really caught my eye, so i worked
to give it centre position in the
image, while ensuring a wide
enough photograph to show the
cold, open floor - GJED

Christ's College

Perhaps the most noticeable thing about Christ's chapel is that it is rather gloomy - there are few windows and it is poorly lit, even in these days of electricity.

But this gloom gives a special flavour to the decoration above the organ console – the face of a cherub. It's more the Renaissance fat baby style than the Bible's scare-the-pants-off-you sort. But during after-dark services it has a "torch held under your face" look to it – rather ominous, and thus much more Biblical. It looks down forbiddingly, especially (and importantly!) at the organist, but perhaps also at all present. Probably few ever notice it – but then how many ever remember the presence of the angels during our worship?

Rev'd Dr Bernard Randall

In here, what little light exists is used to the fullest: Everything, from candle sticks to floor tiles, that can shine, does. To capture this I needed to back off enough to get the windows reflected in the floor - GJED

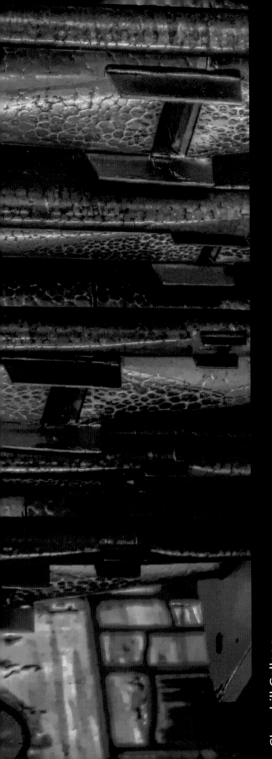

Churchill College

The Chapel at Churchill College departs from the traditional layout of Oxbridge chapels, with their rows of pews facing each other across a central aisle. It resembles more closely a small Byzantine basilica, with the altar placed centrally under a skylight lantern in the timber ceiling. Above the altar and below the lantern is suspended the powerful symbol of a cross with arms to all four compass points. The building's greatest glory is its set of eight intensely coloured stained glass windows, by John Piper and Patrick Reyntiens, which rise from floor to ceiling.

Rev'd Dr John Rawlinson and Dr Mark Millar

Architecturally, Churchill is a departure from the norm, the angles and dimensions are unique and as a result the photographic method had to bend to fit. The range of exposures I used was wider to capture higher range / less tone and I waited until a cloudy day to try to reduce the contrast - GJED

Clare College

I have heard the Antechapel of Clare described as one of Cambridge's finest 'undiscovered jewels'. I agree entirely. It provides a wonderful entrance to the Chapel, and each time I walk in, a great sense of peace and calm seems to descend from the dome. The dome is architecturally remarkable, certainly – but as I gaze up into it, there is a great sense of staring deeply into something that goes beyond the walls of the dome itself, drawing me more deeply into a realm of light. The lantern adds to that by splendidly catching the light and reflecting it, so that, however little light there may be in the sky, even in the depths of winter, the space glows.

Given the embracing octagon shape, it recalls some of the great baptistries of Cathedrals across Europe, and so is a nice link with centuries of prayer throughout the wider church. Furthermore, the Antechapel is an ideal venue for silent meditation and, as Clare, like all the Colleges in the University, is now (rightly) open to students of any faith or none, I sometimes think it provides a safe 'neutral' space for those who are, perhaps, nervous about entering the clearly Christian space of the Chapel proper.

Rev'd Dr Gregory Seach

A great opportunity to catch "golden light" at its finest - GJED

Corpus Christi College

I love the way the light streams into the chapel in the middle of the day, splashing colours from the fifteenth century windows onto the arches and fluid stone mouldings at the east end of the chapel.

Later on, the afternoon sun, shining on the buildings in Free School Lane, lights up our great east window with a luminous glow, highlighting the lovely colours in the glass, giving depth and drama to the crucifixion scene.

Rev'd James Buxton

Corpus has a singular atmosphere among Cambridge chapels. The use of blue accents and the light grey stonework give a very cool, calm feel.

To complement this I needed to wait for a completely blue sky and to ensure that the composition allowed as many of the cooler highlights to show in the final image. In my opinion this image captures its subject chapel's mood as well as any I have worked on - GJED

Downing College

Downing College Chapel was built in 1953, but visitors find it difficult to guess its age. It follows the neo-classical style of the College's architecture, with an uncluttered and simple elegance. It is unusual in facing north, placed along the central axis of the college, and light streams down the aisle from the large south windows.

The Chapel has a beautiful acoustic, making it an excellent setting for choral and instrumental music. It is also a surprisingly flexible space. It feels equally appropriate for a small prayer group sitting on cushions on the floor or for hundreds of people on pews and chairs at a large formal service.

Rev'd Dr Keith Eyeons

Downing was an interesting challenge. The large south-facing windows let in a lot of diffuse light. This smoothes out the texture on the walls and floor, rendering it bland to the camera.

However, it does pick out detail on the complex structures such as the organ and the lectern. So, it was these on which I chose to focus - GJED

St Edmund's College

A favourite feature of St Edmund's Chapel are the four small but delightful stained glass windows in The Nolan Chantry, to the right of the sanctuary. They are dedicated to two great scholars - St Thomas More and St John Fisher - who had the courage to resist a tyrant.

The upper window on the right depicts St Thomas in the Tower being visited by his inconsolable family. On the left is a charming image of the Lady Margaret Beaufort (mother of Henry VII) presenting the great gate of Christ's, the college she refounded, to St John, her confessor; behind her stone masons are engaged in building it. The windows remind us of the integrity and courage that betoken true wisdom.

Rev'd Dr John Kenrick

St Edmund's uses stone in the most functional, least decorative way I have seen in the chapels. To me, the stones here looks alive, useful and the longer you look at it the more colours you see in the rock itself.

I chose to represent this by slightly overexposing the windows, which created a lighter, softer look to the space and allowed the focus to be on the masons' work without a cold, lifeless image - GJED

Emmanuel College

Coming to the chapel each day in different seasons and for different events impresses on me more and more what a genius Christopher Wren was.

The proportions are reassuringly balanced. The expanse of black and white tiled floor exudes generosity and a spirit of toleration while maintaining a feeling of connection. The space never seems too large even for a gathering of just a few people nor too small for an event that embraces the whole College community. The wooden panelling both glows in bright sunlight and enfolds safely in the dark of a winter's day.

Rev'd Jeremy Caddick

The chapel in Emma struck me as golden and it was this first impression I wanted to convey with this choice of photographs.

A warm sun, low in the sky, helped the heavy glass chandelier and grey plasterwork to take on a golden hue from the rest of the building - GJED

Fitzwilliam College

The huge expanse of clear glass on the east side of the chapel offers us a window on to a great plane tree. The two features combine to make a wonderful variation on the traditional stained glass window.

In summer the sunlight glints through the leaves and makes the chapel glow and shimmer. When it is windy we can't help but get transfixed by the branches being buffeted about. At our Sunday morning Eucharist the congregation are prone to stare not at the holy mysteries but the squirrels scooting up and down the trunk and branches!

Of course the tree is also a living reminder of the instrument of Jesus' death. That our rood or cross is to be found outside, sheltering wildlife, challenges us to live out our Christian faith beyond the chapel walls.

Rev'd Dr Tiffany J K Conlin

I wanted to concentrate on the metal and strong angles without creating an industrial vibe, so I waited for a day with strong sunlight to show off the views of the outside world and just underexposed the images a little to take off the glare - GJED

Girton College

I like the sheer presence and architectural quality of the organ.

Some people think it is too big in proportion to the chapel, but it is really a feature of the building, rather than an item in the room.

When it speaks I like to think it is the voice of the whole college, the very stones themselves, trembling and giving glory to God.

Rev'd Dr Malcolm Guite

As the chaplain says above, the striking feature in Girton is the organ. I wanted to show how it was part of the structure of the building.

To do this I made sure it was in the centre of my image and that the light coming from the window behind it was a counterpoint to the hanging lights on either side - GJED

Jesus College

Jesus Chapel's unique delight comes from the combination of ancient worn stonework details from the priory Church of St Mary and St Radegund (the twelfth century Norman gallery, the thirteenth century piscina, the dog-toothing on the piers) alongside the richness of the nineteenth century restorations by Pugin and Morris (the colours of the glass and floor tiles and painted ceiling, the detail of the woodwork).

To pick out any one above the others would be difficult; it is their juxtaposition that is so striking and charming: the medieval survivals alongside re-imaginings of the medieval.

Rev'd Dr John Hughes

What I wanted to capture most from this chapel was the colour.

The rich burnt chocolate colour of the woodwork offsets the blazing windows in way that could only be captured by a wide range of exposures and a wide angle - GJED

St John's College

The eagle lectern appears again and again as a running motif throughout places of worship in England. The College Chapels of Cambridge are no exception.

Originally a reference in wood or bronze to the apostle John, the image of an eagle supporting the bible on its wings comes to have different personal significance for every chapel goer.

Nowhere is this more apparent than in St John's.

As visitors turn from the locked screen preventing their access to the nave they are confronted by a spectacular eagle, rampant and blazing with the thousand colours of the stained glass behind it.

It was that reaction I wanted to portray with the photograph of this college. The long empty chapel with the locked screen and the eagle reflecting the colours of the stained glass.

Achieving the angles needed became the most difficult part of the entire shoot - GJED

King's College

In all the grandeur and over whelming beauty of King's College, with its fan vaulting and stained glass windows, my favourite space is actually one of the side chapels, where we say morning prayer.

St. Edward's Chapel is a calm, intimate space, detached from the busyness of the Chapel as a whole.

Praying there is a wonderful way to start the day.

Rev'd Dr Jeremy Morris

King's is a really easy chapel to take photos of. Any direction in which you care to look, there's a beautiful photo and with that much glass there's always enough light.

However, that itself can be a conundrum. In all that detail and artistry, what view captures the best of the chapel?

In the end I tried to capture as much as I could with a wide view and a select close-up - GJED

Magdalene College

Smaller and more intimate than most college Chapels, Magdalene still has the echo of the small monastic community it once was.

Four statues, recently re-gilded and painted, tell the story of its four saints: Henry VI, Mary Magdalene, Etheldreda of Ely, and Benedict. To sit under their gaze is to be reminded of a living tradition of scholarship, fellowship, and prayer which has been at the heart of Magdalene for almost half a century.

Rev'd Philip Hobday

Magdalene is a small space, and, because of this, a single view can show the overall structure of the building as well as some interesting details. In this case, one such detail is the asymmetry introduced to the image by the structure of western books: leaves being visible on the left pews, spines on the right - GJED

Pembroke College

If you are facing east the visual focus of the Chapel is the painting of the Deposition above the altar, framed by the magnificent arch. This provides a strong background for the Eucharist celebrated in the sanctuary. If you are facing west the visual focus is the lectern, and the organ, with the pews arranged in collegiate style. The emphasis is very much on music and preaching and matches very well the mood of choral Evensong.

If you look closely at the prayer desks on the north side you will see names carefully and deeply carved. They all seem to date from a time when there was no music in Chapel, and Chapel was compulsory. The carving is just out of the line of sight of the Master's seat. Look closely at the cartouches on the wall. There are hidden faces and dogs' noses in the woodwork.

Rev'd Dr James Gardom

The majesty of the stern, authoritarian pillars is countered by the rebellion of the foreground carving - GJED

Peterhouse

The East Window in Peterhouse Chapel makes an immediate impact. It depicts Christ's crucifixion in a manner which is strikingly reminiscent of Peter Paul Rubens' painting, Le Coup de Lance (1618). Some historians even suggest that Rubens may have been consulted over the design. The theological message of the window is quite clear: what happens in the College Chapel, and especially what happens at the Lord's Table, flows as directly from the death of Christ, as the blood and the water flowed from his wounded side. The window is thus a powerful focus for Christian meditation. But the window also bears testimony to the violent religious battles of the past. Defaced by the Puritans during the Civil War, it has been imperfectly repaired since: primitive English glass patching up the sophisticated Flemish original, with faces and limbs ending up in the wrong place. The window is therefore both an inspiration and a warning, and it asks us what shape our own discipleship will take.

Rev'd Dr Stephen Hampton

When given permission to take photos in Peterhouse, it was with one condition: No Tripods.

Balancing my camera on my shoes was not an easy task, but the high shooting angle it forced did lead to the inclusion of that magnificent ceiling - GJED

Queens' College

G. F. Bodley, who designed every feature of Queens' Chapel, supported the Arts and Crafts Movement. Consequently every detail of the hand-carved wood panelling, every bench end, every newel post, every panel above each seat is different. The extraordinary use of colour draws the eye, however, to the east end and the Lord's Table and the inscription over the famous fifteenth-century triptych, set in the sumptuous colours of the reredos, Laus Tibi Jesu Rex aeternae gloriae. I also love the wonderful Pre-Raphaelite Kempe windows, especially the Old Testament scenes. Outside Queens' Chapel seems quite plain; inside it is a riot of High Victorian art.

Rev'd Dr Jonathan Holmes

With so much detail, so much work, it was difficult to pick a feature. In the end, after centering on the blue window to balance the reds, I chose to include as much as I could and let the viewer decide - GJED

Robinson College

Robinson Chapel has an unusual layout and many beautiful features, but the larger of the two stained glass windows is hard to beat for the "wow" factor.

Like many artists of the time, John Piper sometimes employed the imagery of the natural world rather than traditional imagery to speak of the glory of God, and the rich, glowing colours of this window never fail to inspire a sense of joy and awe.

Rev'd Dr Maggi Dawn

Everything about Robinson chapel is odd. The organ, the incredible window, the seating, the structure. The lighting is no exception, so I needed to wait for a crisp, white day to prevent the red bricks from overpowering the image.

It so happened that the best days for crisp, white light were at the end of Michaelmas term, so the photo shows the end of Advent - GJED

Selwyn College

The architectural scholar Nikolaus Pevsner suggested that the altar and Kempe's window above it be linked by an ascending Christ. Karin Jonzen, a Swedish artist, was recommended, and her striking figures now adorn the East end.

They were dedicated in 1958 - the year Selwyn became a full College. I'm fond of the way they draw the eye upwards. But I also like the secret way that below Christ's feet, within the altar, the pectoral cross of Bishop Patteson, Bishop Selwyn's protégé, who gave his life doing God's work, lies quietly. It's as if each knows the other is there, and the movement is complete.

Rev'd Canon Hugh Shilson-Thomas

Selwyn is my college. It's where I learnt to take photographs. I shot this space first of all the chapels and, once I had shot all of the others, I returned to re-shoot the exact same photo, using all of the tricks I had picked up over four years of tinkering with my camera all over Cambridge.

The result is this. This is how I see Selwyn. This is how I saw the woodwork through candle-lit complines and hours of solitary contemplation. This is the atmosphere that returned me to this building in times of need and times of joy - GJED

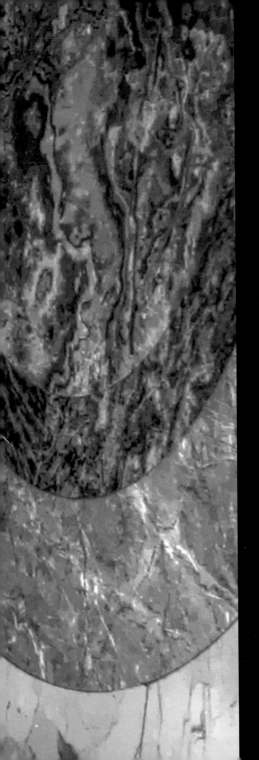

Sidney Sussex College

The best thing about Sidney Chapel for me is undoubtedly the small Lady Chapel, just to the right of the High Altar. It is small and simple in style, with a low curved ceiling. The sacrament is reserved there, on a dark wooden altar, where a red watch candle burns at all times. Above it is a small roundel depicting the Virgin and Child: it is a wonderful place to be still and ponder the mystery of the Incarnation.

Rev'd Dr Peter Waddell

In Sidney I wanted to try to capture some of the details that elevate the simple shape of the building into a much more complex environment. I tried to emphasise the minutiae of the woodwork by standing in a position far off centre and taking an oblique view - GJED

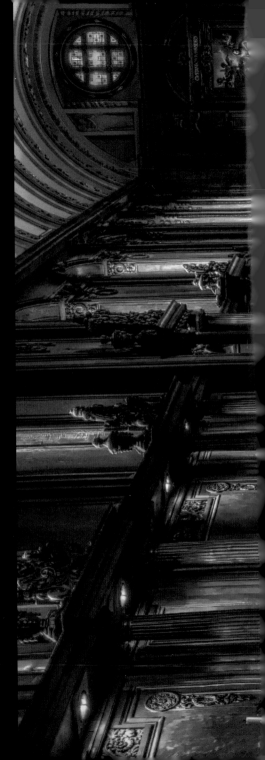

Trinity Hall

Trinity Hall Chapel is the smallest in Cambridge. Little of the original 14th century building is visible and to the eye the interior is early 18th century and deliberately plain.

Tomasso Manzuoli's painting 'The Salutation' ought to be out of place. It pictures the meeting between Mary and her cousin (Luke 1:39-45) at the moment when Elizabeth's baby leaps in her womb in recognition of the Christ-child Mary carries. It fills the Eastern wall with pink, orange and gold colours that should clash with the sombre oak panelling, but seems to bring it to life.

Though the picture's counter-Reformation Catholicism ought to jar with Anglican Evensong, in practice it gives a wonderful visual dimension to the singing of the Magnificat, the song on Mary's lips as Elizabeth greets her.

Rev'd Dr Stephan Plant

What first struck me in this space was the battle between blues and yellows. The tones are all subtle, but if caught on a cloudy day they extend their colour all over the image.

So, all I had to do was wait for a cloudy day and make sure that I got a good selection of dark exposures to bring out the colours - GJED

Trinity College

Every day for Morning Prayer I sit opposite some Cambridge worthies depicted in mid-Victorian stained glass. Two figures in particular bear great personal meaning: the two priest-poets, John Donne (d. 1631) and George Herbert (d. 1632/3). In the window they stand side-by-side, Donne decked in fashionable attire and Herbert in more modest clerical garb.

Studying the two poets in my undergraduate days formed me into my priestly calling. Donne's verse acknowledges the richness of God's creation as well as the possible depths of spiritual despair. Herbert's poetry takes equally seriously our emotional range but focuses on the transcendent hope of God.

These two priest-poets, standing as a pair, are worthy companions in my daily prayer.

Rev'd Paul Dominiak

Trinity Chapel is a huge space. It's really impressive. Light streams in from high windows and gives a misty, ethereal atmosphere. To show the height of the ceilings I took a very low position with my camera. The misty look just came along by itself - GJED

This book would not have been possible without the gracious help and permission of the colleges involved and their Deans and Chaplains. So, in pseudo-alphabetical order, my thanks go to:

St Catharine's College - By kind permission of St Catharine's College
and with special thanks to Rev'd Dr Anthony Moore.

Gonville and Caius College - By kind permission of the President and Fellowship
and with special thanks to Rev'd Dr Cally Hammond

Christ's College - By kind permission of Christ's College
and Rev'd Christopher Woods and with special thanks to Rev'd Dr Bernard Randall.

Churchill College - By kind permission of the Board of Trustees of Churchill College. Warm
thanks to their chairman, Dr Mark Miller and to the chaplain, Rev'd Dr John Rawlinson.

Clare College - By kind permission of Clare College and with
special thanks to Rev'd Dr Gregory Seach.

Corpus Christi College - By kind permission of the Corpus Christi College
Chapel Governing Body and I would like it known that this project would not have
got off the ground without the help afforded by Rev'd Dr James Buxton.

Downing College - By kind permission of downing college
and with special thanks to Rev'd Dr Keith Eyeons.

St Edmund's College - By kind permission of St Edmund's College
and with special thanks to Father John Kenrick.

Emmanuel College - By kind permission of Emmanuel College
and with special thanks to Rev'd Jeremy Caddick.

Fitzwilliam College - By kind permission of the Master of Fitzwilliam College
and with special thanks to Rev'd Dr Tiffany Conlin.

Girton College - By kind permission of the Fellows of Girton College
and with my continuing thanks to Rev'd Dr Malcom Guite.

Jesus College - By kind permission of the Master and Fellows of Jesus College
and with special thanks to Rev'd Dr John Hughes.

St John's College - By kind permission of Rev'd Duncan Dormor and St John's College.

King's College - By kind permission of the Provost and Scholars of King's College
and with special thanks to Rev'd Dr Jeremy Morris.

Magdalene College - By kind permission of the Master and Fellows of Magdalene
and with special thanks to Rev'd Philip Hobday.

Pembroke College - By kind permission of Pembroke College and their Dean,
and my thanks to the man himself, Rev'd Dr James Gardom.

Peterhouse - By kind permission of the Master and Fellows of Peterhouse
and with special thanks to the Dean, Rev'd Dr Stephen Hampton.

Queens' College - By kind permission of Queens' College
and with my hearty thanks to Rev'd Dr Jonathan Holmes.

Robinson College - By kind permission of Warden and Fellows of Robinson College
and with special thanks to Rev'd Dr Maggi Dawn.

Selwyn College - By kind permission of the Master and Council of Selwyn College
and with my heartfelt and humble thanks to Rev'd Dr Hugh Shilson-Thomas.

Sidney Sussex College - By kind permission of the Dean of Sidney Sussex
and with special thanks to that same Dean, Rev'd Dr Peter Waddell

Trinity Hall - By kind permission of the Master of Trinity Hall
and with special thanks to Rev'd Dr Stephen Plant.

Trinity College - Photograph taken by kind permission of Trinity College
and my personal thanks go to Rev'd Paul Dominiak for stepping in to save the book.